Notes for teachers and parents

Equipment needed:

scales
small basin
mixing bowl
dinner plate
fork
knife
tablespoon
teaspoon*
pastry board
rolling pin
cooling tray
pastry cutter (5 cm or 2 in. across)
greaseproof paper
(a piece 10 cm or 4 in. square)
oven cloth
electric or gas oven
(425°F – 220°C – mark 7)
washing-up equipment
timer or clock

*preferably the same size as the 5 ml pharmaceutical spoon

Ingredients needed:

25 g (1 oz.) mixed dried fruit
25 g (1 oz.) sugar
200 g (8 oz.) self-raising flour
½ level teaspoon (2·5 ml) salt
25 g (1 oz.) margarine or butter
milk – not more than 125 ml (5 fluid oz.)
1 egg (Standard or Grade 4)
small knob of lard
butter for spreading

Please tell children that they must seek adult help when they see this symbol:

Put on an apron
and roll up your sleeves.

Wash your hands
and scrub your nails
really clean.

These are the ingredients
you will need.
Put them ready on your table.

mixed dried fruit
sugar
self-raising flour
salt
margarine or butter
milk
1 egg
lard

This is the equipment you will need.
Put it all on your table.

scales	teaspoon
small basin	pastry board
mixing bowl	rolling pin
dinner plate	cooling tray
fork	pastry cutter
knife	greaseproof paper
tablespoon	oven cloth or glove

Set the oven at
425°F (220°C)
if it is electric,
or mark 7 if it is gas.

Turn the oven on.

**Ask a grown-up
to help you.**

Grease the baking tray.
Rub it well,
using the greaseproof paper
and a piece of lard
about the size of a toffee.

Ask a grown-up to show you how.

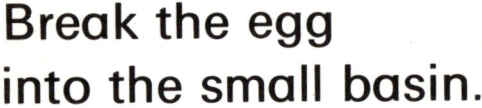

Break the egg
into the small basin.

Add 100 ml (about 5 tablespoons)
of milk to the egg.

Ask a grown-up to show you how.

Whisk the egg and milk with the fork.

Weigh 25 grammes of mixed dried fruit.

Put the fruit on the plate.

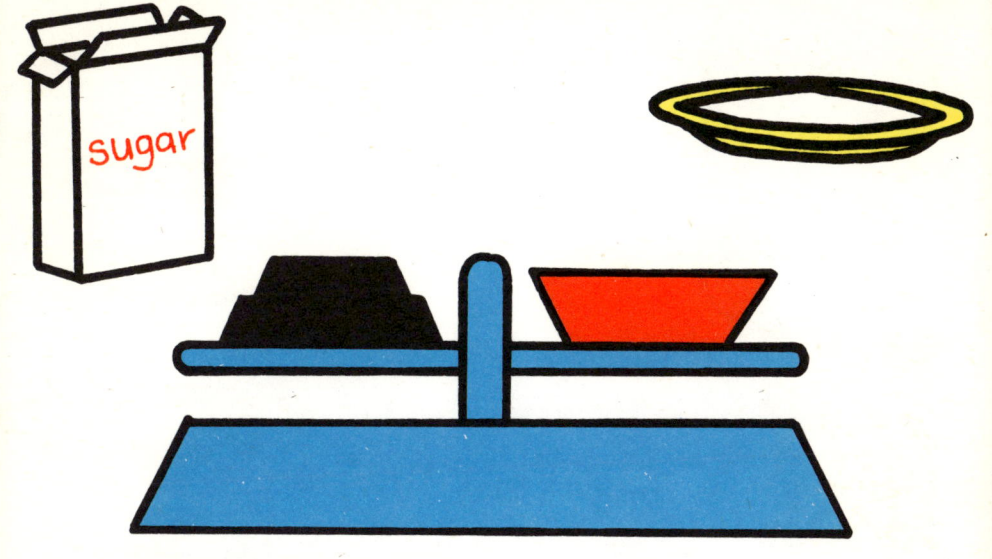

Weigh 25 grammes of sugar.

Put the sugar on the plate.

Weigh 200 grammes of
self-raising flour.

Put the flour in the mixing bowl.

Add $\frac{1}{2}$ teaspoon of salt
to the flour in the mixing bowl.

Stir the ingredients
in the mixing bowl
with the tablespoon.

Weigh 25 grammes of margarine
or butter.

Put the margarine or butter
into the mixing bowl.

Cut the margarine or butter
into small pieces
about the size of a toffee,
using the knife.

Using your finger tips,
rub the margarine or butter
into the flour
until the mixture looks
like fine breadcrumbs.

Ask a grown-up to show you how.

Put the sugar and dried fruit
into the mixing bowl
and mix with the fork.

Sprinkle the egg and milk
over the mixture.
Make a stiff dough,
using the fork.

If some of the mixture is still dry,
keep adding tablespoons of milk
until all the dry mixture is mixed in.

Ask a grown-up to show you how.

Sprinkle a tablespoon of flour
on the pastry board.

Put the dough on the floured board
and make it into a neat shape.

Put a little flour on the rolling pin
and roll the dough out
until it is about this thick:

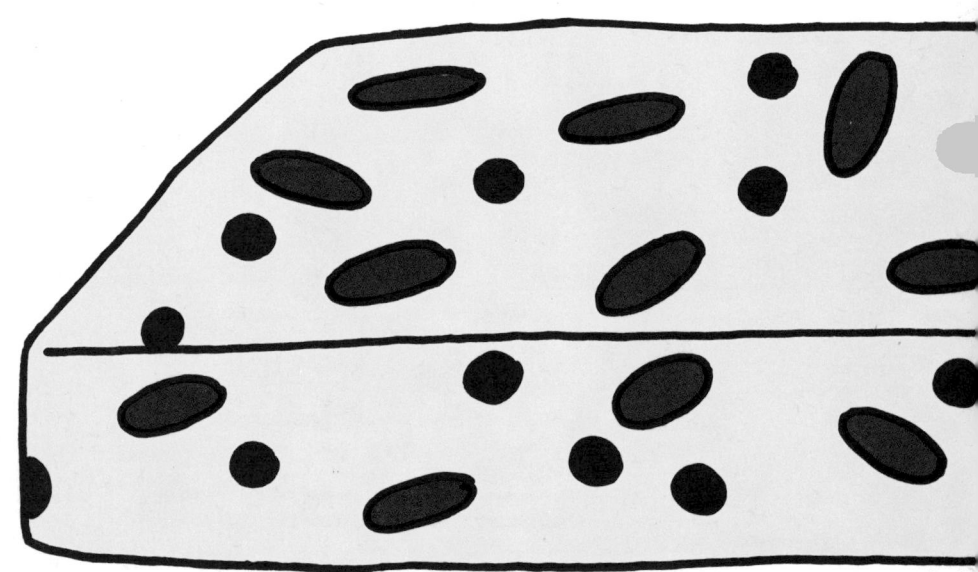

Dip the cutter into the flour
and stamp out the rounds.

Put them on the baking sheet.

Make all the dough pieces left over
into a neat shape
and roll the dough out again.

Cut some more rounds.

Keep doing this
until all the dough is used.

Put the scones into the oven to bake.

Ask a grown-up to help you.

Set the timer for 10 minutes
or check the time
on the clock.

After 10 minutes take the scones
out of the oven
and look at them.

They are cooked
if they are golden brown
and firm if touched.

**Ask a grown-up
to help you.**

Turn off the oven.

Ask a grown-up to help you.

**Lift the scones
on to the cooling tray.**

Wash up
and leave the kitchen
clean and tidy.

Cut the scones in half
and spread them with butter.

Eat!